GOD is not

finished with us

yet !

A Little
Encouragement

Devotion 4 Pastors& Pimps

Written by: **Rod Harris**

FORWARD

I am not a Preacher; I know a few so don't quote me. Do your own research. Get your own Personal relationship with GOD through HIS son Jesus. All I did was break this down the same way I break it down for my friends that aren't saved, that I was hanging with before I got saved and my industry homies that believe but see certain For- Profit Preachers/Churches acting indifferent from the values that Christ showed at times or feel like they don't have time. We are all human and the only Judge is GOD. As followers of Christ our job is to love thy neighbor as you love thyself and love GOD with your whole heart, mind, body and soul. All we got and share the GOOD NEWS. I never read where Jesus said, "Smack them sinners in the face with Revelations (which is a Book of Love by the way)." Jesus understood and still understands people; He was angrier at the Church being a Den of Thieves and trusts me He still is.

Every encounter I had with people who weren't saved nor had one foot in one foot out, I never approached or pounded The Word or passed Judgment. It always came from a place of understanding and forgiveness because I know the World won't give you that but GOD gave me that and I know for a fact "I ain't special." No for real, it's much easier to understand GOD and HIS plan when you read The Word and know it for yourself. You will see how easy GOD made it for us but as humans we always complicate and traditionalize things including The Bible.

So what you have in here are just some things that I feel are important because GOD brought them to my attention. Yep that's right GOD. My Pastor is a Prophet and he is accurate to say the least, he is an amazing person. He told me years ago that GOD would speak to me and when I hear it to write it down no matter where I'm at. So yeah some of this was written in a Walmart parking lot. Some at LA Fitness right after twisting my ankle from literally just walking by the basketball court. A few at the UFC gym on a bench watching these guys kick the brakes off each other and I know for a fact they walked in at the same time, and possibly drove there in the same car. I'm telling you right now watch who you call your friends. So look I hope you enjoy. I hope you learn something and if you do, just know I'm only a vessel. It's all GOD! I can't take any credit.

P.S. I Love You Mom & Pops

Stay Up! Stay Blessed!

TABLE OF CONTENTS

Faith prelude

I still remember the lights flashing in my rearview mirror. I still remember that gut wrenching feeling. I only had this same gut wrenching feeling when I was in Iraq stationed at Camp Cedar 2 in Nasiriyah on our first mortar attack. You never forget it. It sticks with you. You feel helpless. You feel death breathing down your neck and whispering "It's over" in your ear. I remember looking at my wife who was just my girlfriend at the time. I knew it was over for me. As I see the officer approaching the car I tell my wife, "Just say we're going to the casino, that's all." The officer gets to my window and with the most serious and sternest of faces he asks me "Do you know why I stopped you. You were going over the limit let me get your license". I gave it to him as politely as I could. I knew what I had in my trunk was Going to need answers that I didn't have. I can't say anything to them. I have to take the charge. I was running this as a favor for some serious people. So in my mind I'm already preparing to not say anything and own up to it as mine. It didn't take the cop long to come back. My record is clean I knew that no warrants no anything, but I know this isn't my truck. The first thing the officer asks is whose truck is it and to step out so he can search it. I didn't decline and kept my cool so I didn't draw any extra attention to the situation. He searches the inside but doesn't stay too long.He comes outside and walks me to the truck bed which had a locked bed cover on it. He asks if I had the key I told him I did not, I was just borrowing the truck because my car was in the shop. He tries to pry open the truck bed cover with his nightstick but it doesn't budge. Before he tries again, I remember something my Mom told me when I was a child, about having faith in GOD.I knew I wasn't in church like I should of been and that's an understatement I actually hated talking to people who were in to church, I had been running from GOD for years since I graduated High School to be exact. I was the kind of person a preacher or any church goer would avoid at all cost. But deep in my heart I knew the only one who could help me and save me was GOD. So right before he tries to pry it open I said in my heart "GOD save me, if you do GOD I'll serve you forever whatever you want I'll do it" I said it wholeheartedly with no doubt. Not knowing at the time that's how GOD works. That every person in the Bible who ever came to Jesus who came in pure Faith got what they asked for or believed in. As the officer went for a second time trying to pry it open he saw the trash bags and asked what the person does who owns the truck. I said he's in construction. The officer replied" Must be trash he forgot to take out, slow down I'm just going to give you a warning take care of your family." At that moment right there GOD showed me two things. 1: Faith without waiver can move mountains. And 2: I am worth a relationship with HIM. As a matter of fact HE's been waiting on this my whole life. I was so worth it HE sent HIS son to save me even before I knew who HE was. So if you're battling with Faith, this is the book for you.

If "Christians" are not showing you who you really are in Christ, this is the book for you. And by the end of it, my only hope is that you are encouraged in all you do, and realize GOD really wants a relationship with you, no matter where you are at in this thing we call Life.

My hope for you through reading this book is that you not look at this as just another "Devotion" book, but as a sign if you're going through something similar, that it will work out. That you're not the only one who is going through and you won't be the only one to come through. A lot of people have a problem with building their Faith because they think where they are at in life and with no relationship with GOD that they can't have Faith or start believing in GOD to work something out. Through this I think you will see that you have something in common with people in the Bible who got their healing or a circumstance worked out by GOD through Faith. Not only through my testimonies, but through various stories in the

Bible I will point out GOD sent Jesus for everybody, meaning you in whatever situation you're in as well as me. This book doesn't have any judgment in it. I truly believe that is not what we are called to do as believers in Christ. GOD is the only righteous judge. We are to encourage through the GOOD News. The GOOD News will build Faith in a non-believer. Jesus said before He ascended into Heaven thousands of years ago, to go spread the GOOD News. He basically told the people "What you standing here for there's work to do, go tell the people all the good things that The Father has done for us, that Jesus sacrificed it all for everyone." Jesus let it be known that He paid the cost to be the Boss and that we have the easy part...Just believe. It's easy once you get in the groove of GOD's purpose for your life and not your purpose for your life. What is it that you are having a hard time believing GOD for? Did someone hurt your Faith that should of been helping you build it? Do you feel a disconnect because it seems too complicated? Perfect! This is for you even if you said No to every question! Use this as a daily or weekly reminder of things to work on or look out for. Maybe even give you some pointers on how to talk to people about GOD without sounding like you're selling a Pyramid Scheme product. Easy. To the point and quick so it's retainable. If you can retain it, you can reuse in the time of need because you remembered it..it's almost like training for the battle before the fight, instead of needing training when it all hits the fan.

Stay Up! Stay Blessed!

BETTER LATE THAN NEVER.

Acts Chapter 3

Some of us don't know when we actually have a good thing until it's gone. I mean seriously. In relationships, friendships, jobs even Church officials. It's like we're programmed to think there is always something better than what we have and when people feel like that they usually start coming up with false narratives about their current situation to make it seem worn out and outdated or even just bad for their overall condition. I mean think about it like this. Jesus Christ the Nazarene was and is perfect. HE never did anything but good through HIS and our FATHER. All HE did was heal the sick, raise the dead and keep the party going when they ran out of wine. But still these people were blinded by the spirit of stubbornness and thought they were better off in their own sinful nature. That their community would be better off with THE HEALER crucified and a Murderer let back on the streets. They chose to forget about repentance for their sins and choose self-righteousness instead. They ignored all JESUS had done for their family members, friends and even beggars on the streets, and choose to side with the punk pharisees.

Peter was not amused at this. Peter was JESUS' boy. You wouldn't understand that connection unless you have a friend who is the wild card. A friend that would protect you at all cost even if it meant his own life. How angry and real do you have to be to accurately slice someone's ear off. But JESUS knew that Peter would go just as hard for HIM once HE left the Earth. One of the last miracles that was done before JESUS was crucified was HIM healing the ear of the guards servant whom Peter sliced the ear off. Peter could've gotten locked up for that. JESUS saved him!

Fast forward to Peter and John going to a 3:00 o'clock prayer service at their nearby Temple. A man who had been lame since birth was at the

Beautiful Gate as he always were.. When he saw Peter and John, he begs for what he thinks he wants. Like a lot of us who pray and ask GOD for Wants. GOD, I want that new car. GOD, I want that new job. GOD, I want more money. But GOD always gives us what we need. GOD is like; first I need to give you better driving skills so you don't crash the new car, like the old one. I'll show you how to appreciate it and keep it clean and functional. GOD needs to teach you how to be on time and not have an attitude with coworkers so you won't get fired from the job HE has waiting on you. GOD needs to teach you how to save and not be frivolous with your finances so HE can bless you with more. Peter being the standup guy he is, tells the beggar to look at him after he asked for money. Peter said, I don't have any silver or gold for you, but I'll give you what I have. In the name of Jesus the lame was healed. He didn't even ask for nothing after that. When GOD gives you what you need you'll forget what you want. This man held on tightly to Peter and John and began praising the LORD. People were amazed at this to the point Peter seized the opportunity to tell them about themselves.

How these same people could be amazed by this when they have been around JESUS. They chose to crucify the MAN who healed and raised the dead in HIS FATHER'S name. He knew what they did to JESUS was out of ignorance. He told them that. He took this opportunity to teach about having faith in JESUS CHRIST, the Nazarene. They didn't realize they had a good thing before HE was crucified now they realize. But it's not too late, you see they are alive. It's too late when you're dead and in hell. As long as there is breath in your lungs, it's not too late to realize GOD is good and able to forgive. So start today and realize not only is GOD a good thing but HE will never leave you nor forsake you.

Stay Up! Stay Blessed!

SEE THE POTENTIAL IN YOU THAT GOD SEES

(Jeremiah 29:11)

Everybody has plans!Some people have plans for their plans. But all who plan have this in common.. we have no idea if those plans will work. Which is why most of us say, " No worries I'm better at plan B anyway." Who really wants to resort to a plan B? If so, why even have a plan A? Think about how much time is wasted on trying to make plan A work to only have to succumb to plan B. Truth be told that's a trick of the enemy, who is using this as a scheme to get you out of trusting GOD and trusting in yourself. A fact of the matter is saved and unsaved people alike have this same problem.

When you purchase an item that you have to put together you must look at the plans for it and follow the direction from A to Z. Some don't look at the instructions and go off the cover of what it should look like and their own instincts. A large percentage of those people have to resort to plan B when it starts to fall apart because they missed a minor detail that was meant to hold it all together.

Jeremiah 29:11 says "For I know the plans I have for you. They are plans for good and not for disaster, to give you a future and a hope." Wow and to think a lot of us were running in circles not only trying to make plan A B and C work but to make sure they would secure our future, because that is why we make plans for our future. GOD is our creator and HE has made special plans for each one of us that is designed specifically for us that works together for the Kingdom. We do not have to wrestle with our own thoughts wondering what will be of our lives and what our purpose is. The Creator has a masterful plan for your life but first you must submit to HIM. Get off the throne and let GOD be the center of your life. Less of you, more of GOD and watch how he manifest HIS purpose in your life. GODs plans are purpose driven and will give you that sense of fulfillment you are looking for through your own plans.

Yes HE knows our name and yes HE even has plans for you. But right now you must decide, are you tired of plan B's as a result of plan A's not working. We'll try plan GOD and see what HE has in store for you.

Stay Up! Stay Blessed!

GOD HAS A PLAN FOR YOU

Even while in your pit. (Story of Joseph)

Wow. Most of us know the story of Joseph. I actually played a Jailor in the Off Broadway play, "Joseph and The Amazing Technicolor Dream coat." I had to sing to Joseph when he was getting discouraged for being thrown in jail unjustly. Even tho I was in the play there were key points that I missed due to the fact I wasn't searching for anything spiritual while I was on set.

Joseph Father did not notice the resentment his other sons had for Joseph who he showed favoritism to. If so, he might not have sent him to go check on them. But nonetheless he went. He went to where he thought they were at and didn't see them and someone directed him to another town they were at. As they saw him in the distance, they plotted a plan to kill him. I've been in a situation where I went the extra mile to help someone before and they were plotting the whole time on how to get rid of me. I'm sure; I'm not the only one who has been in that situation. GOD sees all and knows all and we must thank HIM for protection from seen and unseen danger.

You see his brothers thought putting him in a pit was a "Pit-Stop" to getting rid of him, but actually GOD was protecting and preparing him for something greater. You see while they had only one thing on their mind, which was getting rid of him, GOD was gonna used him to not only save his brothers but a whole Nation during a 7 year famine. Even when he was in a palace working, Satan was trying to stop him from his calling by using the Master's wife to try and seduce him. It didn't work and she ended up getting angry and falsely accused him. As a result he was thrown in jail. GOD was using this "Pit" once again as not only a "Pit Stop" but as training grounds for his gifts which ultimately got him out of jail and saved a Nation.

My point is doing worry about the Pit. Don't worry how people are taking your kindness for weakness. Don't worry about wicked people plotting on you. Like the word says they are only making a snare for themselves. And no weapon shall prosper; HE did not say it wouldn't form. HE did not say they would not try you. HE promised it wouldn't prosper. So next time you find yourself in that pit. Tell GOD thank you for keeping you and preparing you for something greater.

Stay Up! Stay Blessed!

FAITH: YOU GET WHAT YOU PUT

(Faith Talk)

What is stopping your Faith from growing and flourishing?

Is it because you tried to exercise Faith for something you had your heart set on and it didn't go the way you wanted, it didn't work out, so you gave up Faith in God.

As humans, we put more Faith in humans and have been let down on a dozen of occasions but we still exercise our Faith in the same people who let us down, if that's the case why are we so quick to give up on The Creator? When exercising Faith it's the same as lifting weights. If it's your first time in the gym you don't just put a bunch of weight on the bar and start bench pressing it, you won't get anywhere but hurt. You start off with the bar and

17

lift to get a feel for it so you can learn how to push through in repetitions. The same with Faith. A lot of people are jumping out the window wanting Angels to catch them but have not yet tried just walking with God. Isn't that enough for your Faith to build by knowing you're walking with God (Talk about your vision when you were walking with Jesus and the waves were on both sides). If you know he's with you through the relationship you build on a daily basis, your Faith should be on 100 Trillion. You're Faith, His will and your purpose goes hand in hand for Kingdom Work. Exercise your Faith through your constant and diligent relationship with God. And you don't need an oversized jar of Faith to get things accomplished...GOD knew how hard it would be for a human to trust and to believe in something you cannot see, that's why he said you only need a mustard seed worth. He could've said you need a Palm tree seed size Faith and we all would be lost. Trust and believe just a little and gain a lot seems to me like an awesome exchange. Start speaking in

Faith and watch how it changes your thought process as well. In areas you're having difficulty, speak Faith into those areas. If you're in debt. I thank GOD I'm no longer in debt. Can't find the right companion..I thank GOD for my spouse. Can't keep money in your account.. I thank GOD for blessing my finances. After you speak life into your situation and different areas where you were lacking, start expecting GOD to move on your behalf. Your Faith and GOD's mercy will shift the atmosphere.

Stay Up! Stay Blessed!

The Approach

Turns you on. Or turns you off.

The words in the Bible and lessons you learn through test that turned into testimonies should manifest through your actions. (Not saying we are flawless but chasing His excellence) I know me for example since I just got saved just a few years ago I was in a dark place. Now certain things I used to do like cursing, partying till the sun comes up and seriously SERIOUSLY heavy drinking faded when I started chasing His excellence on its own and not forced. I seriously tried going out setting a "Leave 30 minutes before the club closed" curfew and trying to make it to church the next day. I was making mistakes a newborn is supposed to make but God put someone in my life who knew I didn't know the word but wanted it but I didn't want to feel like I was being condemned. God sent the right person for the task. Who had the word in them and would let it manifest through their walk and actions.

Love and Forgiveness with a side of compassion is how we should approach lost souls. Yes I am a Christian I know you're not saved but how can I help you? How can I show what I am reading in the Bible and other Christian literature through my actions in this situation? Show Compassion for what they are going through. Yes I have been there and He loves you. He just wants you to come back home with Him. I can't curse and damn you to hell for being in the streets unsaved and drinking/ or at the abortion clinics yelling making you feel more hate instead of love because He didn't do that to me when I was down and out, I even need more grace mercy and forgiveness from Him more now that I'm saved than I ever did. "It is easier to catch bees with honey than it is with vinegar." We need to be at these places offering hugs and to say a prayer. And let the people know in gentle tones that He loves them no matter what just come home. You're the child of a great King who will forever reign. You didn't know because the workers are few, but He sent me here to tell you. Out of all the stories in the Bible and I could be wrong but I only remember John the Baptist yelling but he was preparing the way for THE MESSIAH our LORD and SAVIOR JESUS CHRIST.(His matchless name FYI).

Some people could recruit for their job better than they can recruit for the Kingdom, and some don't even like the job they just do it for the incentives. Wow, will you bring someone into something you don't even love but God did everything for you never let you down always came through, (I don't have to know you to know how God comes through for you)and you haven't even tried to tell one of your old friends about what He's done for you. A little bragging on God can do wonders to the unsaved mind. When you talking about what He's done and they see it as well sometimes that's all they need to take you on that invitation to go to church a while ago. They see you didn't give up on them and you hung in there with them even prayed when they needed it all in love because that's what God is and that why He sent His son Jesus Christ to save us.(He rose on the 3rd day like nothing happened and got back to work)

I just want us to approach those who are unsaved as Christ would have approached those who needed HIM and didn't even know it. Jesus Christ didn't turn His back on those who needed Him; I mean even if you touched the hymn on His back you were good. There is no other God but our God and we are His children. We must love and not judge for He is the judge we are not He is up there we are down here. No one is better or bigger than anyone. Show them the love and Turn them on to Him. What if Jesus acted like some modern day Christians? Who would be worthy to be saved?(Compare Jesus approach to modern day Christians) What if the beggars and lepers who wanted to be healed by just touching Jesus clothes were told by Jesus. Oh heck no look at your clothes plus I don't know you like that to help you? What if

Jesus never corrected his disciples about children and how to have their Faith to enter the Kingdom? What if he agreed to the people stoning the woman who committed adultery instead of telling them "He without sin may cast the first stone?" What if he never took time for the blind man at the gate? What if he never ate with corrupt tax collector?. Well he might be just like a lot of Christians now a-days which is why when one church official does something wrong the world comes and attacks the whole church. Because we teach forgiveness and mercy but only show it to those saved. And you wonder why Jesus cracked a whip in church and not on the streets with the sinners. They don't know any better but we do and we must show the same Love Mercy and Forgiveness we want from GOD to everyone saved or not.

Stay Up! Stay Blessed!

"DON'T BOTHER JESUS!"

They say(Faith Talk)

Some people feel they can't receive Jesus as their Lord and Savior because of their current state of sin and how other Christians look at them or side eye judge them.

• I have yet to read anywhere in the Bible where Jesus or GOD says to be already good and clean when you come to them. But I could be wrong I haven't read the entire Bible cover to cover.

• The punk Pharisees were church officials who side eye judge everyone even side eyed Jesus so let that digest real quick if they did JC like that obviously they don't have it all together.

Run to Him, he's waiting on you

• Don't go to GOD half speed go full speed. HE's been waiting on you forever. HE's literally been waiting on you your whole life. Facts. I know me when I'm waiting on my kids to get out of school how excited I am because I know what I have in store for them. So like the word says " If you sinful people know how to give good gifts to your children, how much more will your Heavenly Father give good gifts to those that Love HIM." -

HIS healing power is for the sick, broken-hearted and sin filled person who is ready to confess and receive HIM into their heart

• All through the New Testament when someone was healed it was because of their Faith. Their bold walk up and find Jesus in my worst state Faith is what healed them. Them came to HIM full speed.

• The Roman Officer had whole hearted Faith. Zaccheus seen Jesus and confessed wholeheartedly. The paralyzed man had faithful friends who didn't let a crowded house or roof stop them. The woman with the issue of blood had that I don't care what the law says about my disease I just need to touch the hymn on HIS garment Faith.

My daughter was in Intensive Care right after birth, GOD healed her so fast they were confused at the Hospital.

• And what do all of these people have in common, they experienced his healing power First hand and gave GOD the glory for it. Not modern medicine or thought they body just healed itself like Wolverine. Don't keep what GOD has done for you from people, the last thing Jesus commanded was for us to go and share the good news. Your healing is good news. Your new look on life after you get saved is good news. You made it through whatever situation you and everyone thought you wouldn't make it through, is Good News.

Understand this is a trick of the enemy who knows that there is only one way to the Father and that's thru the son. It's in the Word and the enemy knows the Word as well. Satan doesn't want to you to be healed by the blood of Jesus. He knows that's the only way to be forgiven truly. I think of all the times I would miss Church before I got saved and think now, "Man Satan really tried to kill me before I got to the Son to prevent me from being reunited with my Father?". Say for instance you needed something from me and you come knock on my door. My son comes to the door and says Hey whatever you need just let me know and I'll get my Father. Instead of greeting my son you spit on him, curse at him and even tried to kill him. What do you think I as a Father will do? This is what certain religious leaders and people did to Jesus when all he came for was to help and save the world.

Jesus wants you to come as you are physically mentally and spiritually. He knows what's needs to be fixed. Some people think Church and GOD are only for those doing good and looking their best. Always smiling and not a care in the world. Hmm well if that is true why was Jesus hanging with the Thugs and degenerates. Crooked Tax collectors and Ladies of The Night? Oh yeah that's right those are the ones he was sent for. The ones with needs. The ones with hurt and pain they can't hide.

Somewhere along the way Christians forgot why Jesus came and what we should do as his representatives. Do you Christians not know how many people you have sent to hell by how you have treated them? Do you know how the homeless view a lot of the church? Well I'll tell you this if they stopped believing in GODs mercy it's because how a lot of us walk around with our nose in the air not even looking to have a conversation with the woman at the well. Some of us don't even talk to people in church unless they are familiar so quit acting like your talking to the people unsaved at your job. And I'm not talking Bible Thumping. What verse did Jesus say to unsaved people? He made sure he had something that made sense. The Bible calls it Parables, and since a lot of Christians seem a little confused just find something you can compare to and quit acting like you been saved since birth and never needed the same Mercy and Forgiveness unsaved people need. Truth be told saved and unsaved alike need the same Mercy and

Forgiveness from the same GOD. So that means we all need Jesus.

(Remember)

Sin will have you doing things that you said you never will do. Faith will have you doing things you never thought you could do.

Stay Up! Stay Blessed!

CLEAR YOUR HOUSE.

Receive Your Miracle(Mark 5:35-43)

1st of all Jesus is in rare form in this time. He was on a healing streak. The man with a 1000 legions just got healed. The woman with the issue of blood just got healed. And now it's Jarius time to see for himself. If this was an NBA Jam game they would say "He's on fire" Jesus was showing out and removing doubt. Not to mention he just calmed a whole storm before getting off the boat. Jarius came right on time. I mean Jesus was powering up on the haters and punk Pharisees. In the midst of his conversation with the woman with the issue of blood, some people came from Jarius house telling him his daughter had died and don't bother Jesus anymore. Y'all tripping Jesus is the exact person you need to bother when your situation is dead and these are perfect conditions for a miracle.

Notice Jesus kicks everyone out except the Parents and his Disciples, his boys who have all the Faith from seeing Jesus work miracles in the last 24 hours and the parents who are in a desperate situation who believe Jesus is the only answer the only solution for their problem. Also notice what Jesus says before he kicks everyone out. HE calls things as tho they should be. The Pharisees thinks Jesus is tripping when HE says the girl is just sleeping. They see things for what they are. Another problem in the Christian community. Too many believers who don't believe in miracles. Too many saved people who believe where your at in Life is where your always going to be. No wonder Jesus kicked them out. After the saved non believers leave ..Jesus does HIS thing as usual and the little girl wakes up. Once again GOD is bigger than any problem and Jesus was practicing conquering the grave.

Some Christians are like this girl, you can't receive a miracle because of the so called saved ones around you who believe in GOD but don't believe in change for you. They believe in GOD but they believe more what's right in front of their eyes. They only see the problem and not what it could be with GOD as the solution. Don't be embarrassed to clear your house and only keep those who not only can touch and agree but whole heartedly believe that GOD is going to change your situation from Death to Life. Think of all the people who came to the Pharisees for help and all they seen was the surface of the problem and gave no hope no prayer just threw the towel in. We don't serve a throw the towel in type of GOD. HE doesn't even know what that means. And if more Christians understood that maybe the world wouldn't be in shambles like it is. Maybe more healing would happen at Church. Maybe more healing would happen in your community. Maybe more people would get saved. Clear your house tells all the people who don't believe your situation can rise again, tell em they gotta go. There is only room for people who believe in not only me but most importantly that GOD isn't finished with me and my dead situation is about to come back to life. (no matter your situation If Jesus was walking on this Earth as he did long ago he would tell you"Don't listen to them, trust me."

Stay Up! Stay Blessed!

NEVER 2 GOOD 4 SINNERS

(Luke 19 1-10)

• Too many times in the New Testament you notice Jesus has no problem or issues with sinners who want to know if he's real. Not talking about the punk Pharisees who only tried to trap Jesus, but actual sinners who are curious about the life they are living in contrast to the way Christ was living and teaching. Zacchaeus was one of the blessed ones who were able to see Jesus face to face and just being in Jesus' presence warranted change. We'll call him Zacch for short. Zacch was shorter than the rest and could not see over people's heads in the crowd, so he ran ahead and climbed on a tree on the path were Jesus would have to walk by so he could just see the Savior. (Hold up. This sounds like me). This was a Matthew 7:7 moment where you keep on seeking and you will find. When our big brother Jesus approached the tree, He called for Zacch to not only come down, but Jesus informed him He would be staying with him that night. And as usual, when Jesus did as our FATHER would want us to do people started mumbling about Jesus staying with a sinner. They thought Zacch was a notorious sinner. But Jesus knew he was the exact candidate that needed to spend time with Jesus. And all the while as the people worried about Jesus' moves Jesus knew His moves would move Zacch, because the light will always push darkness out. Almost instantly, as Zacch was in Jesus' presence, he started to confess his wrongs and also divided a plan to pay back those he wronged and to help the poor.

• Jesus knew all his wrong doings and shortcomings but did not even have to mention them. All he did was show genuine interest, compassion and the willingness to fellowship with someone who others deemed not worthy. Wow! Jesus' approach is so perfect. While some Christians won't even talk to you if you look different, dress different, or talk different. (Or just because you are not saved.), imagine if Jesus did that while he was on earth. What if He only talked to priests at the temple. He would have no disciples, no water would get turned to wine, thousands wouldn't get fed from 2 fish and a loaf of bread, and the man with legions of demons would still be screaming. I often see these practices in small groups at mega churches who group you with people who have the same interest or in the same age bracket. It somewhat teaches you subconsciously to stay with what's familiar and not to venture out into unknown territory in the name of spreading the Gospel.

• Imagine getting saved and turning your back on the ones you use to run wild for Satan with. Don't they deserve to see the light that now shines through you? Notice I didn't say they deserve for you to go back and preach on why they are sinners. Sometimes the most effective ministry, is your life. We'll call it the' "Zacch Ministry". Show interest and love for a person so genuine and authentic that they just pour out to you what's wrong, because they see you as a comforter which is only there because of GOD. Remember the ones watching are not always there to see you doing wrong like the Pharisees, but often times they want to see how real it is in your life because it's a change they long for.

Stay Up! Stay Blessed!

FAITHFUL WARRIOR

(Faith Talk) 1 Samuel 17

David wasn't the underdog. Goliath was. I wish preachers would tell the story right. One GOD never puts you in a situation where you will not be victorious no matter what's in front of you. Rather it's a Lion's Den, a Fiery Furnace or a Giant that only scares those who don't know the Creator. Goliath brought a knife to a gunfight. He was preparing for hand to hand combat, and David was a sharp shooter. David had a sling not a slingshot. Slings in the hand of the right operator are very dangerous weapons.

GOD uses what you have in your hand and what you are already familiar with, because HE knows unfamiliarity in a war can get you killed. The things you have already defeated have prepared you for this great battle against your Goliath. We are always in a spiritual war.

Goliath, in anyone's situation seems like a difficult task, but in all actuality, they are the underdog. When you have a relationship with GOD because HE,will use what's physically in your hand and spiritually in your hand to defeat any enemy, because your Faith says so. GOD will turn an impossible task into one that is easily done and executed. Where Kings and soldiers get scared, GOD will raise up a Faithful warrior in you. Be like David. Claim your victory through Faith right in the face of your Goliath.

Stay Up! Stay Blessed!

Don't Hide You from Them

(You are the biggest witness)
Romans 3:23-24

Don't hide who you are from unsaved people, because sometimes them seeing you as a human who is flawed, but striving for excellence, can be the biggest testimony to them. You might can reach someone the Pastor cannot, being in places they are not but representing GOD in the correct manner. Not perfection which most of the world confuses us for being and some Christians even think they are as well, is a dangerous area to trot around.

You may be the only representative of the Kingdom that they encounter. GOD is depending on you to represent not only the Kingdom but, HIS mercy HIS love HIS forgiveness; not HIS judgement. Which a lot of Christians feel they are the right arm of GOD in the flesh, not knowing everyday we all need the same love ,mercy, and forgiveness that comes from the same source. Saved or unsaved, every day we need the same forgiveness. "Oh we don't you say? Mr. and Mrs., I sit in the front row every Sunday."

Romans 3:23-24New International Version (NIV)

23 for all have sinned and fall short of the glory of God, 24 and all are justified freely by his grace-through the redemption that came by Christ Jesus.

So now that there is a verse to back it up, do you understand that you have something more in common with an unsaved person? What if GOD acted like you and denied a chance for forgiveness and mercy and HIS love. Doesn't feel so good does it? For some reason we feel we are the only ones entitled to this. We are not entitled, nor do we deserve it, but that's our FATHER being merciful beyond measure. Always there for us, and we dare deny the unsaved this opportunity? But we do.

When we hide who we are. Broken vessels. When we hide our source of redemption and mercy. The FATHER and the SON. Think of all the lost souls you have encountered and had a chance to be a witness to them, but you didn't. You hid who you were. You hid behind the false idea of perfection the church provided, as if they were not a club member, so access to the SAVIOR was denied. Sad. Truly sad that you forgot we are to be the extension of GOD. The hands that should reach out to them and pray. The arms that hug the broken-hearted and wounded. The feet that run to meet needs of those in need. The ears that hear wrong and the mouth that can comfort and speak up for those falsely accused who cannot defend themselves.

As a community and family, we must change our way of thinking. Stop thinking it's all good because you have your salvation. That's great. But who else that you know or love has this golden ticket that you hold privately? Does anyone unsaved around you know how to receive theirs or is your mission accomplished. For some of us saved, it's a good thing we won't recognize people in Heaven, because a lot of y'all wouldn't know anyone up there other than Biblical characters or famous people. You won't recognize anyone in your circle or family because you hid who you were and did not afford them the opportunity to the Kingdom. Oh it's the Pastor's job to get people saved? My bad! I forgot that part in the Bible were it says " Pastors are the only ones who can spread the good news and bring people to Christ." Must be in the "Too Good for Sinners", version of the Bible. Sorry, I don't have that one, nor do I care to read it.

It's truly the end times that our Grandmothers told us about. We have no time to play with people's souls. We don't have that kind of time. Every second, every minute, every hour, every day, every week, every month, every year matters. And we don't have time to play the blame game or point fingers. There is only time for Mercy, Love, and Forgiveness. So go out and represent your Father and the Kingdom, correctly. Souls are depending on it. Heaven is waiting, and Hell is mad that souls that would occupy it, are being turned around. Snatching them straight from the gates of Hell, just by being you. (Sinners are made right in HIS sight when they believe in HIS son ,Jesus Christ).

Stay Up! Stay Blessed!

Thankfulness Prelude

In Dec 2006 I returned back from Iraq. After a mandatory VA appointment, I was diagnosed with Post Traumatic Stress Disorder. It comes with a whole host of other issues mainly depression, which I have been battling for years. At this time I wasn't in church and I started self-medicating which is common for returning Combat Vets. This includes mixing the pills they prescribe with drinking and partying until early in the morning it's a way we vets mask the pain shame and hurt we experienced while in combat. During this time I stayed away from church and anyone associated with it because I felt no one understood what I was going thru. Imagine being so low and so depressed that the only way you feel things will get better is to kill yourself. A few times I loaded my 40 cal and put it to my head and would cry. Other times I would leave the house and call my wife and tell her to hide the guns before I come home because I feel I'm going to shoot myself. But GOD had other plans. I have a praying Mom who was concerned so she had my cousin Tonia invite me to Covenant, I can't remember what was preached that day but I remember standing up when they asked who would like to be saved. GOD walked with me to the front and I met brother Don. He shared that he also dealt with depression. He suggested to not only give just money but my time. And also to write a journal. The first page I wrote was depressing and it made me look at my life and get more depressed. At this time I was reading a passage of scripture that said that GOD didn't want our burnt offering he wanted our Thankfulness, so I decided to try that. Instead of writing what I was going thru I started writing what I was thankful for. I found myself self-medicating in Thankfulness. My atmosphere was changing and I started seeing myself as GOD sees me; special and loved. To this day I'm battling depression but I have medicine that works faster than any pill created and I don't find myself depressed for months or weeks at a time anymore. Suicidal thoughts don't control me like they used to, and I am Thankful for that. What are you Thankful for?..

Stay Up! Stay Blessed!

WISDOM FROM GOD

Use Wisely (1 Kings 10-11)

A lot of times when I pray I often ask GOD to give me wisdom, not wisdom so I can go around and brag about being wise or smarter than other people but wisdom to help HIS people. The word says our people are destroyed for their lack of knowledge or wisdom. So obviously it is important for our survival that we seek Heavenly wisdom and not earthly wisdom. Wisdom can be used for great things for the Kingdom but in the same token people can use wisdom for their own personal gain and notoriety and sometimes to get over on people who are not as wise. Wisdom from GOD is not to be used to impress men. It's supposed to be used to help those in need.

At some point before Solomon started not using his wisdom for good that he received from GOD, he was using it for the good of the people so they could see GOD working through him. He was a great judge at one point even figuring out who was the rightful mother the child belonged to. His wisdom was impressive to other King's and Queens of foreign lands. Unfortunately, all that wisdom eventually went to his head. He forgot why he asked for wisdom and who granted him riches in return. Often, a lot of us (when things start going great), we forget who is the sponsor of all this greatness. Who is responsible for our joy and freedom, our peace and provision, and who is the author of it? When this happens we must expect things to go down hill.

Solomon let things distract him from GOD... actually it was women. He was King but his nose was wide open and he had no self-control. He was not in control. He was not the priest of his household. He allowed foreign women to make him worship foreign gods. He didn't do it in private, but disobeyed the GOD who gave him everything openly. In return the kingdom was ripped from him.

We can't point fingers at Solomon because we are like this at times too. We get going in life, and after we pray and GOD delivers to us quicker than Amazon, we forget the conditions we were in, and often start to pat ourselves on the back after people start to sing our praises. Let them sing praises. We can't control them but don't let it gas us to praise ourselves and not the Creator. Learn from Solomon. It won't end well. So, today, if you are in the same situation as Solomon. You prayed for a promotion got it and didn't thank GOD, but went out with your friends to party and celebrate instead, don't let them gas you when you know it was all GOD. Go to GOD let HIM know you're sorry for Giving yourself credit when it was all HIM. Thank HIM and regain your favor.

Stay Up! Stay Blessed!

What's Your Issue?

(Luke 8:40-48)

For those who have a bank account they understand you have to go to the bank and get your money. You have to physically get up and go to the bank to receive your cash. When you have an issue that requires finances you have to physically go there and get your cash. Disregard your credit cards and cash paying apps, we are talking about things that require immediate cash or immediate results.

Jesus was a walking ATM. Automatic Transformation Machine. And the people knew this, which is why the crowds were so big when HE was around. Huge crowds with no gaps. You were literally standing on top of people to see Jesus. People pushing with excitement and request. Some just to see how real HE was and some for request. It was sometimes chaotic and even more difficult when you have physical ailments that can hinder you.

Enter the lady with the issue of blood. In these days people with these types of sickness could not be in public. It was against the laws of those times. She knew all of this, but her Savior was in the vicinity. The One who can heal the sick, raise the dead and make the blind see is in the area but it's against the laws of the times for her to interact with the healthy, but healthy people don't need a doctor.

As she steps outside she sees the humongous crowd and thinks "What are the chances of him being able to stop and talk and lay hands on me to give me the healing I need?" Zero to none. Jesus was walking through a crowd that looked like a mob. She thinks to herself, "If I could just get close enough to touch HIM, I will be healed".

She guides her way through the rough crowd. She's losing blood could possibly be dying. She goes high and low, but can't seem to get close enough to touch his hand as everyone is reaching for Jesus. As a last resort she reached as far as she could in Faith and touched the hem of HIS garment. Not the sleeves, not the front or back piece of HIS garment but the hem. Instantly the bleeding stopped. Jesus stopped because HE could feel healing leaving HIS body going to someone, but HE did not lay hands on them. "Who touched me?" Jesus asked. HE knew who touched HIM but HE was teaching a lesson in Faith. Everyone denied it and Peter assured to Jesus the whole crowd is touching HIM. But Jesus wanted to know who touched HIM in Faith. She fell on her knees trembling and explained why she touched Jesus. I can imagine Jesus smiling as HE said, "Daughter your Faith has made you well go in peace."

Awww man, do you know what this means for us as GOD's children? Healing is all in your Faith. So when you reach for GOD for healing don't let anything get in your way or sidetrack you. Don't let the large crowds of non-believers determine your

Faith. Don't let a crowd of Christians determine your Faith. Let your Faith be that as a child. Let your Faith be perfect. Reach at all cost for Jesus and I guarantee you will leave in Peace.

Stay Up! Stay Blessed!

Faith or Fear

How Do You Operate

As humans we all only operate in one or 2 ways when faced a difficult task, situation or a place of unfamiliarity and uncomfortability.. it's Faith or Fear. Some psychologist call it fight or flight. But since we know it's a spiritual war at all times we're gonna call it what it is man; Faith or Fear. You either believe GOD brought you here so HE will bring you out or you forget all HE has done to get you where you are. The Israelites went 2 days without finding water. Literally ,they just walked through a sea of water to escape Pharaoh's army and now they are complaining instead of praying. Really y'all, as soon as we come across a bitter creek or something not suitable to our likening we panic instead not only thanking GOD for keeping us but sustaining us. Imagine every situation every disagreement, every discomfort, every brokenness. Every hurt is an opportunity to

Faith it so you can face it instead you fear it now GOD can't clear it.

The Israelites went through unnecessary things all because they were lacking Faith. Won't be the last time they would drink bitter water; I can tell you that right now. Now my man King David (before he was King) was the perfect example of "Faith It". Joseph and Mary are perfect examples of "Faith It". Daniel in and before he got in the Lion's Den..that's right you guessed it "Faith It". I look at these things as the impossible so I know my situation no matter what it is ain't nothing to GOD. If y'all realized nothing you got going on is bigger than GOD you would Faith it more than you Fear it trust me fam.

GOD is a jealous GOD ,so you can't "Fear it" and "Faith it" at the same time. It's either one or the other. When you're not in your word and don't have your own personal relationship with GOD you're more than likely in that Fear zone. Think of it like being in the Friend Zone. You're gonna get jealous when you see other people in this great relationship with GOD that you could of been in but you can't let go of Fear to experience the Faith life. Can't get nothing from GOD like that. And it doesn't take much Faith just a little and no Fear what GOD has planned for you. Not saying you won't have human feelings and be uncertain about new things. But as soon as those feelings arise say to yourself or out loud whichever applies at the time. " I know GOD got me so you know I'm not even worried." Watch what that little proclamation can do in a big way.

Stay Up! Stay Blessed!

GOD BETS ON YOU. EVERY TIME

1 Corinthians 13:7 (Faith Talk)

GOD is Love. Agape love. The kind that doesn't give up. The kind that will search far and wide for HIS lost children to bring them home where they belong. GOD never gives up, GOD never loses Faith, is always hopeful and endures through all circumstances. The world only knows how to bet on you when you're winning but when your down they always count you out. The world will even beat your or kick you while you are down. The world doesn't know love like GOD knows love. The world would want you to think that love is in the club drunk grinding on you. The world would want you to think worrying only about yourself is love. I've been there thinking this was love, but when you're down and out this kind of love can't help at all.

But GOD is the real Love. HE doesn't see you at all how the world sees you. HIS love is there in the day to guide you and at night to comfort you and to dry your tears. HIS love is everlasting. And not only has that GOD bet on you in every situation. Imagine that when your facing your challenges and turmoil. GOD already bet on me to win. Wow that feels great. Knowing GOD knows all and HE is betting it all on you.

Stay Up! Stay Blessed!

GODs Body Armor

Eph. 6: 10-17

When I first heard about "Putting on the whole armor of GOD", I thought it was something only seasoned Christians could do. Like you had to be at level 50 in Christianity and GOD would send you a care package to defeat the enemy like in a video game. That you had to have this perfect walk with CHRIST and you had to pray for hours fast for a year and then like a video game this care package of Body Armor would appear on your steps like a package you ordered from Amazon. I would think, "If GOD really wants me to succeed at defeating the enemy why isn't this easier to obtain? Doesn't HE know all the trials and temptations I'm going through to reach level 50?". Oh HE does. And HE hasn't made it hard to obtain HIS armor..we have. If the US Army can issue gear and your Kevlar armor prior to mission prior to being deployed and not when your in the fight, then how come GOD didn't issue it before our walk? HE did! You weren't paying attention you're like the guy in my unit who missed getting his TA-50 because he didn't pay attention to the announcements about it. Before the beginning of time GOD knew who HIS children's fight was going to be against. HE knew of the evil rulers and authorities of the unseen world, the mighty powers in this dark world and the evil spirits in Heavenly places and HE was prepared for it before we were here.

Belt of Truth: GOD wants us to stand firm where we are at in our life, and what's the easiest way to win an argument, The Truth. The truth is like building your house on a solid foundation. It will weather every storm and make you always stand firm. The truth is your belt. You can always tell the truth, always.

Body Armor: GOD's righteousness will always protect you. It covers you in times of attacks. GOD's righteousness is forever. But we must keep that relationship with GOD always thanking HIM, and always praising HIM for what HE has done in our lives.

Shoes of Peace: you have to have shoes, so why not walk in peace? Peace that surpasses all understanding. Do you even realize how much different you walk when you have peace? Do you realize how different you walk when that peace comes from GOD? It will make your chest poke out and your head held high. Peace will fully prepare you for things to come. No matter what happens around you, Peace will comfort you because it comes from the Good News. The Bible is filled with good news.

Shield of Faith: Picture that punk Satan with a little bow and arrow. He'll shoot a fiery arrow of self-hate of depression, of isolation, of fear, and lack of finances. Will you hold up that shield of Faith when he fires and block it. If he fires self-hate arrows, you block it with the faith that says GOD loves you and you're important to the Kingdom. Block it, block it ,block it, and speak things in your life through faith and ignore those arrows from that punk.

Helmet of Salvation: I feel it's one of the most important pieces of armor because it's your mind and satan is constantly trying to win that so he can destroy you. When images and thoughts come in your mind that is not godly you speak against it. Ask GOD to cover you with the helmet of Salvation or a simple "Jesus help me and protect my mind". Sword of The Spirit: Aww man, the Word of GOD is the greatest weapon of all. When it's time to attack because your tired of the enemy attacking this is what you use. A lot of people don't know the word so they are constantly under attack because they have no offense. What you eat will come out of you so I encourage all to eat the word. Claim it, Announce it, when Satan is attacking you let him know you are not to be played with and you have something for him if he keeps it up.

None of this is because we earned it or deserved it. GOD wants us to be prepared at all times. HE gave us an alarm system called, "The Spirit of Discernment" that will make us aware of a spiritual attack. Pray for yours. GOD wants to give us wisdom. All we have to do is ask and our gracious Father will give it to us. So understand GOD's armor is not issued to you at a certain level of Christianity. You can obtain it. HE wants you to.

Stay Up! Stay Blessed!

Staying Righteous

(When Evil Men plot on you) Story of David vs. King Saul (1 Samuel 18-19)

Have you ever been hated on and plotted on by someone who all you've tried to do was help? Have you ever worked for someone who was a jealous Boss? Even though it seems like they have everything, they act as if you have something they want as well. It's your Peace that passes all understanding that they want. It's the favor that GOD put over your life that they want. They can see it. They just can't achieve it and it bothers them.

Before David was King he served King Saul. David was an anointed Shepard. He was anointed by the prophet Samuel. Not only was he a warrior, he was a musician. He was brought to King Saul to play his harp to soothe the King as he was being tormented internally. Even after that David came to King Saul's rescue again when GOD used David to defeat

Goliath and save the lives of Israelite Soldiers from death and slavery. Even after this, it was not enough to keep King Saul happy. When people shouted David's name as a hero, it hurt the Kings pride. Even after defeating an army, David still played his harp to soothe King Saul, who with an angry and jealous rage, tried to kill David with a spear. Even after that David forgave him because he was a Godly man and trusted GOD.

This story continues in an almost Roadrunner and Wile E Coyote style. King Saul chased and GOD provided David an escape route and kept him safe until it was time for him to be King. I've been there I'm sure you have been there, where the person you work for seems like they have good intentions for you but behind closed doors they are jealous of your work ethic. They dislike that other coworkers like you more and sing your praises even though that is not what you tried to accomplish. You can't help that glow GOD put on you. You can't help you have GOD's favor. So what do you do when evil men in charge plot on you? You remember this verse, "No weapon formed against me shall prosper." Be like David. Be resilient. Be forgiving. Be encouraged. The same GOD that got you to this point can bring you not only through it, but on top.

Stay Up! Stay Blessed!

GOD WILL ALWAYS PREPARE (TRAIN) YOU

For what's next (Story of Young David the Shepherd).

With GOD you never finish where you started or what you started as. When you seek the Kingdom certain things happen in your life that you could have never imagined or prepared for yourself. I could not of told you at age 8 what was in store for me 24 years later, but GOD knew and prepared me better than I could, even if I knew. When I was an alcoholic, GOD was preparing me even at that moment to be an encourager. When I was a fornicator and a cheater, GOD was preparing me to be a relationship counselor. But most importantly, GOD sent HIS son Jesus to prepare a way for all HIS children of every race on every continent. GOD is the great preparer and HE sees you as a warrior and King. Even in your "Shepard stage" he prepares you.

If David was told that he would defeat a mighty warrior giant even before he slain a lion and bear, that might of discouraged him because he never knew what it was to kill something that could kill him to get to his flock. He might of even been in disbelief. But after killing a lion and a bear he was prepared not only skillfully but mentally. My first night on Force Protection detail in Iraq I ran 3 insurgents down on foot who broke the wire and were on their way to do soldiers harm. I didn't even hesitate when we got the call. l took off with one of my Soldiers. I was prepared. I trained in Korea as well as the states for something like this. My E-6(next shift leader) just sat there scared no training. He wasn't ready for that. I was prepared.

GOD is like a good father. A good father knows he needs to prepare his children for the harsh realities of the world. HE gives you chores to prepare you to work and appreciate what you have. He sees what's ahead and prepares you today. Goliath thought he was a big boss when he was fighting David's people, but he had no idea that GOD prepared a Shepherd boy years before to protect what was close to him from all kind of wild animals. Not talking coyotes and hyenas..we're talking Lions and Bears..no matter how big and strong and scary Goliath or his crew of flunkies thought he was..nothing is more scarier than a hungry bear or lion coming to attack your flock. But that's nothing when GOD is at the head of your life. HE's got you no matter what seems to try and overwhelm you GOD will have you so prepared that when people try and help you will be able to decline their help because all you need is what you've had all along to defeat the enemy. GOD prepared you with something you're already good at. David was good at killing animals to protect his herd. And Goliath in his eye was no different than the lion or bear trying to kill his flock. In fact David had a righteous anger in him against the giant who dared to insult GOD. GOD will prepare you for every battle you have to fight and every race you have to run. HE's there every step of the way getting you in order and prepared for your mission. Some say "Trust the Process".. I say Trust GOD so you can enjoy the process.

Stay Up! Stay Blessed!

LIVING AND DYING 4 CHRIST

So who will fight?
(1 Samuel 26-32).

Today as Christians the story of David should be confidence a builder in this fight that we are in, as we look around and see the world defying the commandments of the One True Living God. Making their own new normal and turning foul living into righteousness in their own evil hearts. We as Christians have made turning the other cheek into not getting involved or not engaging this culture of sinners to spread the message of Love and Forgiveness to them. We have stopped witnessing to those in need of God and started witnessing and sharing testimonies with those who are in communion with God because we are scared of conflict because we think it's not Godly. What is not Godly about standing up for God? It should be more of a sin to turn the other cheek in situations where you should be standing and fighting. Don't get me wrong, there is a time and place for everything. A time to pray (all the time) a time to rejoice, a time to engage, and a time to wait. So, when is it a time to fight? If we asked David, he would most likely say, "When they outright defy the Armies of Living God and his people." Some Christians are facing their own Goliath's, but instead of having faith and remembering who that Goliath is defying and stand up and fight they act like scared Israelites who forgot all the victories God gave them time and time again(Never Forget). In this day and age God needs warriors like David, Samson,Ehud,Joshua, and generals like Deborah to lead the fight against these Goliath's of infidelity, hate, racism, idolatry, fornication, alcoholism and all other Goliath's the evil one sends our way. Who will stand and say "Don't worry about this Philistine, I'll go fight him!" Who will put their Faith on display for the enemy and not waiver? Who will decide to live for Christ before it's time to die for Christ? You will, you faithful warrior.. Again, there is nothing wrong with wanting to die for Christ. It's an actual honor, but don't let that be your first option especially if you haven't exercised the option of standing and living for HIM...we have enough Christians who have already laid their swords down and are out of the fight and some who's relationship with GOD has died and you're just going through the motions..and to them I say "Rise up". Just like GOD raised a dead Army that were all bones he will raise up your beyond dead relationship and give you life and more fight in this war on principalities and spirituality... You will live for HIM. You will fight for HIM.

Stay Up! Stay Blessed!

REAL FRIENDS

(Mark 2:1-12)

Who are your friends? Are they willing to go the distance? Sometimes we all need that push that gets us over the hump. Some of the time we have that drive and do not need the help. But other times we need friends like the paralyzed man had. You see they had the faith. They knew their problem solver was inside but the entrances and exits were packed. So what did they do? They went the distance. They didn't let a little thing like not being able to walk in to see Jesus deter them from what needed to be done. They climbed on the roof and did the unthinkable; they started to dig in someone else's roof to make a hole big enough to lower their paralyzed friend down to the Redeemer. I'm sure as the digging started they probably heard people saying things like, "What are they doing?" "Couldn't they just wait until some people left to try and get in?" and "Are they crazy digging into the roof?" That's what we need sometimes; friends that don't care what people are saying about them (who some might think are crazy) and who won't wait to get you the help you need. But overall Faithful who believe in something just as much as you believe and will not only pray with you and believe but are willing to do the work. I'm sure their paralyzed friend heard Jesus was in town but maybe got discouraged knowing he couldn't walk to see HIM. That's when their Faith kicked in and they didn't let a little thing like being paralyzed stop their friend from seeing Jesus or even a packed house. Do your friends have this kind of Faith? Do your friends push for you when you feel you have hit a dead end? Do your friends carry you when sin paralyzes your thought process? Do your friends pray? We all need these types of friends; friends who don't care what the obstacles look like ahead of them because they know the Redeemer has the answers and they will push through to get there.

Friends (3 Sets of Friends)(Faith Talk)

The Prodigal Sons "Friends" - Friends who are only gonna be there when it's good.

They come out of nowhere only to take and leach on to what was gifted to you. They have no intentions on repaying you or at the least helping you like you helped them especially in your time of need. They're always on the scene but the scene is not theirs. They go from opportunity to opportunity like the wind blows a leaf. Never stable. Never secure.

Job's Friends- Stuck with him and wouldn't let him blame GOD for his problems. Was there to talk with him. Although they did question him for questioning GOD they didn't let him blame GOD and ultimately he begged for GOD's forgiveness. Sometimes your friends have good intentions at heart but don't understand what GOD's plans are for the bigger picture.

The Paralyzed man's Friends- Not only are they with you till the end, and not only are they tired of talking about it, they are willing to tear things up to get you the help you need and deserve. They are about that action, they are with results, and they were and who can give them. They are Faith Warriors and are willing to pick you up and Faith you to Victory. Some people are in a paralyzed state with Job friends or the Prodigal son friends. They are not gonna pick you up and get you to where you need to be to get right. They're gonna talk your ear off and not even be there for you.

Some of us are in a paralyzed situation in life with Jobs friends. All they are gonna do is talk about what you need to do that's not who you need. in this situation...some of you guys are going through a season like Job, and all you had were the prodigal sons friends, and they are never around for you. As a matter of fact they, got up out of there before your well dried up.. and some just don't know who their real friends are because of who they are or what they have. Let GOD pick your friends for you. Ask for a spirit of discernment so you will feel who is for you and who is against you. It's all principalities and spiritual at the end of the day so ask your gracious FATHER for wisdom and watch HIM grant it.

Stay Up! Stay Blessed!

MUST BE PERSECUTED

In route to prosperity.

J esus knew how important His mission on earth was. But He also knew in order for His people to prosper He must be persecuted. The definition of persecution is to be on the receiving end of hostility and ill-treatment, especially because of your race or political or religious beliefs. Jesus was not greeted with open arms like He should have been everywhere He went. In all actuality there was always a group of haters, called Pharisees that didn't have a spirit of discernment to know that Satan was just using them as tool for hate on GOD's only begotten son. But He still kept on with the most important mission ever in history; to die for us even though He never did anything wrong that even deserves this type of persecution. In all actuality we are the ones who deserve to die like He did. Jesus only deserved our praise and thankfulness but He ran toward His persecution

81

with little questions asked. Matter of fact He only talked to God about it the night before He was to be crucified.

So who do you think you are to think that you will only experience joy and not pain, sunshine and not rain. The Bible states that the rain falls on the just and the unjust alike. I should blame the Church for this actually, who teach prosperity 11 and a half months out the year and rarely talk about Revelations during revival week. The first chapter 3rd verse in Revelations states "God blesses the one who reads the words of this prophecy to the church and HE blesses all who listen to its message and obey what it says, for the time is near." But I guess a lot Pastors look at Revelations as judgement and not a blessing, and think it might scare the congregation, to bad they don't know it is a book of Love.

Prosperity without persecution is unrealistic. You can never make it to the ranks of CEO without making your way through the company totem pole. Persecution brings wisdom and strength to get you to where you need to be. If my dad had babied me and loved on me all the time and had been there for me I would of failed at life when I was homeless and hungry. It would of been almost like a culture shock to go from silver spoon to all of a sudden fallen on bad times. My skin would have been too soft to make it through the ringer. He didn't know GOD was using him to prepare me for my destiny and persecution was part of it and as I look back on it I am thankful for my father and how it prepared me.

If you received your gift without going through something to get it, how can you truly enjoy it. How could you truly protect it if you do not know the dangers of the world. You would be unprepared, less skilled and it would vanish from your hands like thin air. Your persecution prepares you in more ways than one. So next time your going through it, thank GOD for preparing you and getting you ready for your blessing through your persecution.

Stay Up! Stay Blessed!

THE HONOR CODE

Ephesians 6: 1-4

Too many times I have heard people who do not want to comply with what you're saying or their ego is too big to see someone is helping them utter the words," But you're not my Dad, you're not my Mom!" I too was one of those individuals especially in the Army and in College. If I didn't agree with you and didn't care to understand what someone was telling me, those were usually the words that would come out of my mouth usually. It was as if my parents were there it would of changed the outcome of my decision. Not at all. I didn't honor my parents either. I felt they were the enemy, especially since me and my father's relationship was null and void. The way I was provoked by my father it caused me not to honor him and my days were not well.

The scripture is a commandment with a promise. You see GOD knew what becomes of a child who is disobedient, and does not honor their mother or father. GOD knows what happens to a child who is provoked by their fathers. It's a long road of things not going well with you because a lack of respect for authority. GOD gave us Fathers to provide, protect, and to provide provision for their children. Your father's actions should reflect his relationship with GOD our Heavenly Father. Our Heavenly Father and earthly father work hand in hand to help us complete our Kingdom Mission while on Earth.

Think about it like this if you can't respect your biological parents or guardians how will you ever respect authority. How can you respect something you have no blood ties to if you don't even respect your Father and Mother. Your lack of respect will cost you things like, opportunities to advance in you job or career. People won't help you like you think they should because they know you won't show respect.

When I wasn't listening and honoring my parents life was rough. My credit was bad. I had to file for bankruptcy before I turned 22. I was homeless. I had no foundation. No wisdom. I was a leaf blowing whichever way the wind took me. Life was not well with thee. It was downright harder than it had to be. I was also running from GOD at the time. I had to honor my parents and that doesn't mean get in your knees and kiss their feet and shower them with gold and diamonds even tho some parents might think that would be nice. No I had to honor and understand my father's flaws and how it affected how I was raise. I had to appreciate and thank GOD for how it was and how it made me become a better Father. I had to honor what he did right how he kept a roof over my head food in my stomach and clothes on my back which is a hard job and doesn't come easy. Most of all honoring my earthly father gives the praise to my Heavenly Father because GOD knows I trust HIM with who

HE puts in my life. GOD makes no mistakes but our most common mistake as Christians is not trusting GOD completely with our life only the things we feel are out of our control. Truth of the matter is everything is out of our control the only thing we can control is our Praise our Thoughts and who we choose to honor.

Stay up! Stay blessed!

COME IN AT THE BOTTOM

Leave on Top (The GOD way) Story of Daniel and Friends (Daniel 1)

I know a thing or two about being evacuated from where your form into a new place with no familiarity. My family was evacuated from Panama in December 1989. I remember that night. I remember the lights being turned off in the Airport and all the families having to get on the ground. I remember being rushed to the C130 on the tarmac. I remember hearing the bullets hit the plane. Then I remember landing in North Carolina, December 24th, Christmas Eve with nothing but a suitcase and what we had in our book bags. We lost everything and now we're in a place that is unfamiliar.

So this story of Daniel and his friends Shadrach, Meshach, and Abednego that my mom use to tell me always stick out to me because of the vague similarities of being in a different land not knowing what will become of you next. They marched nearly 900 miles in captivity from Jerusalem to Babylon. But upon arrival, GOD showed favor to them as they were picked to try out for the royal court. They were given the best of life inside that palace. GOD put these righteous men who still prayed 3 times a day in comfort. Like I've been saying ..Your pit, is just a pit stop. They were wise enough, to not eat the food that was blessed by the priest to foreign gods. You know the make believe ones that never rescue you, or listen to you, or provide for you. They only ate veggies and water, the original vegetarians, and they were smarter wiser stronger and faster than all the others. But not only that GOD was setting them up to be officials in the royal court. One night King Nebuchadnezzar had a dream that disturbed him. A dream only GOD could interpret. He turned to his trusted advisors none who were righteous none who feared the one true GOD none who prayed to GOD. Only GOD could show the King and interpret the dream. But HE used Daniel and his 4 Friends as an influence on the Kingdom. The King threatened to kill all the wise officials if they couldn't tell his dream. But Daniel asked the King for a night so GOD could tell him his dream. The King granted it(Favor).

That night the 4 Friends touched and agreed on it, and GOD showed them the dream not only to spare their lives, but to use them to influence the Kingdom again, Favor. Needless to say the next day they interpreted the dream and the King was happy. So Happy he acknowledged that GOD is above all GOD's(HE's the only one FYI) and also made him ruler over all Provinces in Babylon and ruler over all the wise men lives he saved..more favor.

So you have to understand it's not where you start or even if you are an foreigner in an unfamiliar land or an immigrant escaping a war torn country and seeking refuge . GOD qualifies you GOD gives you Favor. It's not up to men to give you what GOD has for you. It's on you to stay the righteous course and for GOD to bestow the favor on you. Notice I didn't say perfect course. Only one man ever walked the Earth was perfect and that was HIS son my homie my big dog JC. So understand it's not where you start or how you start it's all about how GOD finishes it for you.

Stay Up! Stay Blessed!

HE DIDN'T GIVE UP ON ME

I won't give up on you.

How can you give up on your children?

I see and hear it so often, Christian parents saying they did as much as they can do or that's all they can take when their children don't go down the path that they are taking. The moment that child steps outside of what you have taught them and if they are old enough, they get the boot or a back turned to them. And then we wonder why they love the world so much. We wonder why they get into the world they talk about us to the world. Then we wonder why the world, in turn ,talks down about God and call us hypocrites. We as Christians can't even forgive and show mercy like God has done for us to our own. What if GOD got tired of forgiving you and showing mercy, and thought you were old enough to understand and gave you the boot? Or even turned HIS back to us? Not a good feeling, actually it's the worst feeling. We must be a liaison for GOD's Mercy and Forgiveness. We must be the not only a light to world but we must be that light that's willing to go the distance in the darkness to bring them out. We must sacrifice ourselves like GOD sacrificed HIS son, perfect awesome and matchless JESUS CHRIST. Be quick to listen slow to speak slow to anger and quick to forgive and show mercy.

Stay Up! Stay Blessed!

NOW IS NOT THE TIME TO HIDE

(Sauls Prophecy) Samuel 8-10 (Devotion)

Never be scared to your calling when GOD called you to do it...yeah we gotta start it like that. I know me after my meeting with Lenny S. when he was at Def Jam...I can still remember how to get to his office, after you go left when you get out the elevator. He loved the music. Showed me the difference between a radio record street record and club record. My numbers were subpar and I would have to get them up on social media. Show everybody who I was with, where I was at. Basically the money and the lifestyle which we were actually living at the time but never needed to do it for the Gram..I ran from it fast. It pushed me in other directions but I definitely ran from one of my callings. Jonah did the same thing at first. It cost him a couple days in a beast belly but it also got some people saved. But Saul was already anointed by Samuel who is the person you want to anoint you, you would think it would be smooth sailing at least in his mental department..not at all. Not only was he anointed by Samuel he was given a prophecy as to what will happen that day to confirm the prophecy. You would think that would be enough to stand strong. Sometimes in our human nature to run and hide from a situation that we are not to familiar with and scares us. Saul isn't the first person this happened to and it won't be the last. It doesn't say what he did while hiding in the luggage or even how long he was in there. But you have to imagine how scared someone has to be about their new found position as King. Sometimes what GOD has for you can overwhelm your flesh, especially when you know what you have been through and especially when you still see yourself as the world sees you. It's hard to accept the role of a King when the world has treated you like a peasant your whole life. It's hard to see yourself as married when you've been treated bad in every relationship. It's hard to accept the role of a counselor when you have been the one counseled your whole life. But if you can just for one second imagine everything that you think your not and imagine GOD saying you are. You are worthy of a great relationship. You are worthy of the new position at your job. You are worthy to get that new house. You are worthy not because of yourself but because Jesus paid the cost. Now get up out of the luggage you have a kingdom to run.

Stay Up! Stay Blessed!

JUST BE STILL AND KNOW
PSALMS 46:10

You know a lot of times as People we tend to not tell what's really going on when people ask because of fear of rejection. A lot of people don't want to be around any negativity and you know it so usually when someone says "What's up" you usually say "Nothing Much". Us as Christians take it up a notch anytime we're asked how we're doing. Man I'm blessed and highly favored, knowing your going through a storm that can be overcome where 2 or more are gathered in HIS name. Now I'm not saying that your only being real if you tell others your problems or what to pray for. Not at all. Because your Gracious Father knows what you need even before you ask HIM. So when a time like that appears just let your brother or your sister know when they ask "How are you doing" just say I'm being still.

There will come a time when you don't know what your doing you feel like your in a neutral place. Your not doing bad. But your just here. Existing. Not really living life abundantly. At times you may even see and think people who did you wrong when you walked away from a situation where they took advantage of you because they know you are a Christian. Just know that HE is GOD. No matter how your situation feels like your just not going anywhere never let it frustrate you. Relax and know that the same GOD that got you through and out is the same GOD that has you Still for your good. For your purpose. And for HIS glory. Be still and know that HE alone is GOD and HIS plans to keep you safe from seen and unseen danger. In the midst of the stillness you will have rest strength and understanding. So don't worry that everyone else in the world is moving at speeds that your not. Trust GOD has a plan for you even through your stillness.

Stay up! Stay Blessed!

THE IRONY OF THE
CHURCH

But those who won't care for their own relatives, especially those in their own household have denied the true faith. Such people are worse than unbelievers. I Timothy 5:8

While I was stationed in Iraq during Operation Iraqi Freedom, every now and then we would perform something called "Peacekeeping Missions" to the local villages in the Nasiriya area. Giving supplies such as but not limited to freshwater, MRE's and various other goodies we receive(even fixed a bike for a local) to the Local Nationals (LN's) in that area. I always wondered why is that we haven't done any of these peacekeeping missions in the States, in various communities around the country. It seemed as if it was easier to help others before we help our own. It's like society, even the Church makes it a point to pour help and ministries into foreign countries when our own country is in need of help in certain parts, and all are deserving of the same ministries we are putting overseas. I've been in churches that will raise hundreds of thousands of dollars to help the Philippines Cambodia and other countries that are getting aide but not even help volunteer to help feed and clothe the homeless down the highway. I've seen people come to Christ and get saved in church one day and we as a church say all the nice things to them and comfort them to the altar, then not help same person who just lost a job has no car with a wife a 2 kids. It's almost like we are bad Salesman. You know the ones in the middle of the mall in the kiosk trying to sell you a new phone or hair and facial products. We say whatever to get your attention we get it sell you the product and you never hear from us again. Do you not see the danger in that? Do we not see how that can cause resentment to the church? We must not only help bring souls to Christ but we must do "PeaceKeeping" missions in our own communities and churches to keep them and their souls from backsliding. We must always display the full Love of God. Which is to love thy neighbor as thyself. I love myself enough to feed and clothe myself therefore I love my neighbor the same when I see they are in need. How can I go to another neighborhood after a storm and offer my help when I have not helped my house or even my neighbors. We as the church must do all we can to show God's love and our faithfulness through good works by taking care of those in needs. The homeless the elderly the widowed and the deformed. For God is Love and we are His Children , The Representatives of that.

Stay Up! Stay Blessed!

God sees the Paul in you. Not the Saul

Acts 9:1-18(s2)

I was once watching the coats or belongings of people who persecute God and his people. I once took pleasure in the things that were detestable to God. I would run away from anyone who had a good word to give about the glory of God. I was on my own throne and only about my kingdom. Now that I think about it I was exactly like Saul. I was raised in the church and was taught to fear and love God. But when I left home I became all about I and the works and pleasures of the evil one. See he knew I was searching for love and an eagerness to fit in with any and every one. Even through all the fornication, drunkenness, unfaithfulness and evil deeds God seen the Paul in me. Even better than that all things I was going through would not be in vein but to be used to help others who are going through the same things. How beautiful and wonderful is that?! No a blinding light did not knock me off my high horse but a serious conviction brought me to my knees in tears in the midst of sin. Almost as if the conviction was saying "Rod! Rod! Why are you torturing me?" God knows our turning point. Destiny and purpose must be fulfilled and God knows both. There were times where I surely should of perished not just in Iraq either. But God knew that Paul would rise up in me and stand firm one day and on Gods time. Even when I was in my Saul ways God showed me his Mercy and Protection because he knew that one day I would get to the crossroads of life and make the most important decision in my life..and that would be to stand up and walk tall for him. He used my mom to plant seeds even when I was of this world. She would always call me "Mighty Man of God" and I didn't understand at the time I never spent time with God I only prayed when I ate and maybe before I went to bed and the only Bible verses I knew were John 3:16 and a verse that said "Jesus wept". So how could I be this Mighty Man of God like Paul? God knew that like Paul one day I would arise up from my sinful ways and stand firm on his Word and let it be known that this world has nothing for you or me because I was about this world and not Him. When a preacher who has been saved since he was 8 talks about fornicating or clubbing and hasn't experienced it, it comes off to someone who is stuck in that life or living that life as condemnation instead of help for deliverance. Like when I was acting like Saul how could I talk about God I would be a false teacher and a fool. God knew that my Saul(ful) ways would one day be used to deliver someone from the Devil's grasp and see the bright light from God who just wants to put you on the blessed and righteous path. I thank God for protecting me while I was Saul but praise and bless his name for seeing the Paul in me and having it manifest in my life.

Stay up Stay blessed

We All Just Have To Do Our Part (Quick Reminders, Pick Me Up or Pep Talk. You decide)

Chase His excellence. Not perfection.

Let Him change you and don't tell others what needs to be changed. Tell them ask God to change what needs to be changed.

Enjoy. Understand. Embrace. The process.

We are all here to spread "The Good News" of our Fathers miracles that He has done for us.

If the church took out their own traditions and beliefs and go back to what God says everything out here would be much better. The world doesn't influence the church. The church influences the world.

You have to remind yourself what God has done for you in times of discomfort and grief. Don't become Israelites who Thought God freed them from Egyptians to die in the wilderness. He was building their faith up in order. When they got to the Promised Land they should destroyed those giants but their faith was too small. They should of been a whole bunch of David's by then and stepped to the Giants in Faith.

When you stay War ready you don't have to run and pray in the midst of the fight or intrusion all you have to do is stand firm. A lot of Christians are caught off guard by calamities when the enemy comes to plunder your household because they are not standing firm some are standing on their own understanding instead of God's.

Stay Up! Stay Blessed!

GET SAVED

(Repeat These Words)

Father I love you for loving me when I didn't even love myself

Thank you for your forgiveness Father

For I am sinner who repents for my sins against you Father

Thank you for sending your only begotten son so now through him I have a way to you Even tho I'm not worthy of your love Thank you that you eagerly pour your love into my life and for that I am ever thankful

I love you Father so now I ask you to come into my life and shift the atmosphere renew my mind and heart

And Thank you for always being there for me

I ask you to let me join your family

And I also ask Jesus to write my name in The Book of Life

Amen
1 Chronicles 7:14

(Tag your It.)

Made in the USA
San Bernardino, CA
06 May 2020